Brush with Greatness
Pierre-Auguste Renoir

Amie Jane Leavitt

CURIOUS FOX BOOKS

© 2025 by Curious Fox Books™, an imprint of Fox Chapel Publishing Company, Inc.

Brush with Greatness: Pierre-Auguste Renoir is a revision of *Renoir*, published in 2017 by Purple Toad Publishing, Inc. Reproduction of its contents is strictly prohibited without written permission from the rights holder.

Paperback ISBN 979-8-89094-166-4
Hardcover ISBN 979-8-89094-167-1

Library of Congress Control Number: 2024949112

To learn more about the other great books from Fox Chapel Publishing, or to find a retailer near you, call toll-free 800-457-9112, send mail to 903 Square Street, Mount Joy, PA 17552, or visit us at *www.FoxChapelPublishing.com*.

We are always looking for talented authors. To submit an idea, please send a brief inquiry to acquisitions@foxchapelpublishing.com.

PHOTO CREDITS: pp. 2–3 (background)—Shutterstock.com/Mr Twister; p. 16 (map)—Shutterstock.com/olenadesign; All other images—Public Domain. Every measure has been taken to find all copyright holders of material used in this book. In the event any mistakes or omissions have happened within, attempts to correct them will be made in future editions of the book.

Fox Chapel Publishing makes every effort to use environmentally friendly paper for printing.

Printed in the USA

Contents

Chapter 1
Madame Renoir   5

Chapter 2
Mixing Paints   9

Chapter 3
Studying the Masters   13

Chapter 4
Painting a Painter   17

Chapter 5
Home Sweet Home   23

Timeline   28
Selected Works   29
Further Reading   30
Glossary   31
Index   32

Luncheon of the Boating Party feels both busy and calm at the same time.

CHAPTER 1

Madame Renoir

"That's me holding the dog." Madame Renoir **(muh-DAHM ren-WAHR)** pointed to the lady in the painting. "This one is called *Luncheon of the Boating Party.* That was when I first met my husband. He included many of his friends in this painting."

The painting was very big. It stretched nearly 6 feet (1.8 meters) wide and 4 feet (1.2 meters) tall. I wasn't quite that tall yet, so the painting was bigger than me!

My neighbor, the great artist Renoir, painted it many years before I was born. It was definitely one of my favorites. I enjoyed looking at it

every time I went to the Renoir home. I always saw new things in it, just like that day. I hadn't known Madame Renoir was in the painting!

After studying the painting with her for a few minutes, I asked, "Is Monsieur **[mis-YUR]** Renoir in his studio?"

"Yes, Leo," she replied. "He is waiting for you."

Aline Charigot (ah-LEEN-ah SHAR-ih-goh) was a model for some of Renoir's paintings, including *By the Seashore*. She later married him.

Self-Portrait was painted when Renoir was 34 years old.

CHAPTER 2

Mixing Paints

I walked down the hallway toward Renoir's studio. As I entered the room, I saw the great artist sitting in front of one of his latest paintings. I had never seen him out of his wheelchair. He could walk a little, but it was very hard for him. He said he wanted to save his energy for painting.

"Leo, you are here!" he said excitedly. "The paints are on the table. Will you mix them for me and then bring me my brush?"

"Of course, Monsieur," I said as I hurried over to the table. I found his palette, just where I had left it the day before. I put dabs of green, yellow, and blue on the wooden board. I placed the palette and brush into Renoir's hands gently. His hands had bandages on them.

It was hard for him to hold things anymore, but he painted anyway. I was there to help him set up.

"Arthritis **[arth-RY-tis]** is a terrible disease, Leo," Renoir said. "But I'm determined to keep painting no matter what. Even if it's harder. Thank you for helping me by mixing my paints."

This was one of the things I liked most about my neighbor. He never quit, no matter how hard things got. I wanted to be like that, too.

Self-Portrait was painted when Renoir was 69 years old.

The Skiff uses small brushstrokes and lots of color to show a scene.

12

CHAPTER 3

Studying the Masters

As Renoir painted in his studio, I walked the halls of his house. I liked looking at the paintings on the walls. As I gazed at each one, I imagined I was painting them myself.

I looked at the bright colors of *The Skiff*. Sunlight sparkled on the lake. There were many different shades of blue in the water. There were also strokes of white, pink, red, and yellow. Even though it didn't look exactly like real life, I could tell what was being painted.

"Monsieur Renoir learned to paint by studying other paintings," Madame Renoir said as she came down the hallway. "He spent hours and hours at the Louvre **(LOOV). **That's an art museum in Paris. He would look at the paintings there. Then he would try to paint his own to look like them."

"Did he begin by painting on glass? I heard someone say that," I said.

"You heard right. My husband did not come from a rich family. When he was 13, he went to work. He was the apprentice **(uh-PREN-tis)** to a porcelain **(POR-suh-lin)** painter. He painted pictures on things like dishes and fabric fans. But my husband wanted to do more with his life. He wanted to be a serious artist. That's when he started taking art classes, where he met Monsieur Monet **(moh-NAY)**. You remember meeting him when he visited, right?"

"I sure do!" I replied. After all, who wouldn't remember meeting Monsieur Monet? He is a famous artist just like Renoir. How lucky I am! I am so young, but I have already met two of France's best artists.

Many of Renoir's paintings look very soft, such as *Young Girls at the Piano.*

This painting uses mostly blues and yellows, yet the scene is still clear.

16

CHAPTER 4

Painting a Painter

At lunchtime, Renoir took a break from painting. I put the brushes and palette away and wheeled him into the garden. I set a tray of croissants, cheese, and grapes on the table. Madame Renoir joined us. As we ate, Monsieur Renoir talked about the old days.

"I loved living in Paris. It was the perfect place for a young artist. I spent days painting along the Seine **(SEHN).** That is where Monet and I came up with our style of painting."

I nodded, excited to hear more.

"Critics called it impressionism **[im-PREH-shuh-nism]**. This is because we showed the impression of a scene. I don't need to paint every detail like a photograph to get an idea across. Other painters joined us. We were all such good friends back then. We even put together a show of our paintings. That is when people really started noticing us."

"I remember Monet when he showed me the painting you did of him!" I said to Monsieur Renoir.

"I did several of Monet," Renoir said. "I think he showed you the one of him painting in his garden. I liked the idea of painting a painter as he painted."

Renoir laughed. Madame Renoir and I joined him. That was a clever idea!

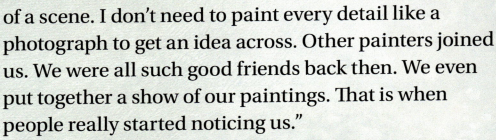

Monet Painting in His Garden at Argenteuil **(AR-john-tay) shows the artist painting a real work, called** *The Garden of Monet at Argenteuil*.

Dance at the Moulin de la Galette (MOO-lahn day lah GAL-eht) is Renoir's most famous painting.

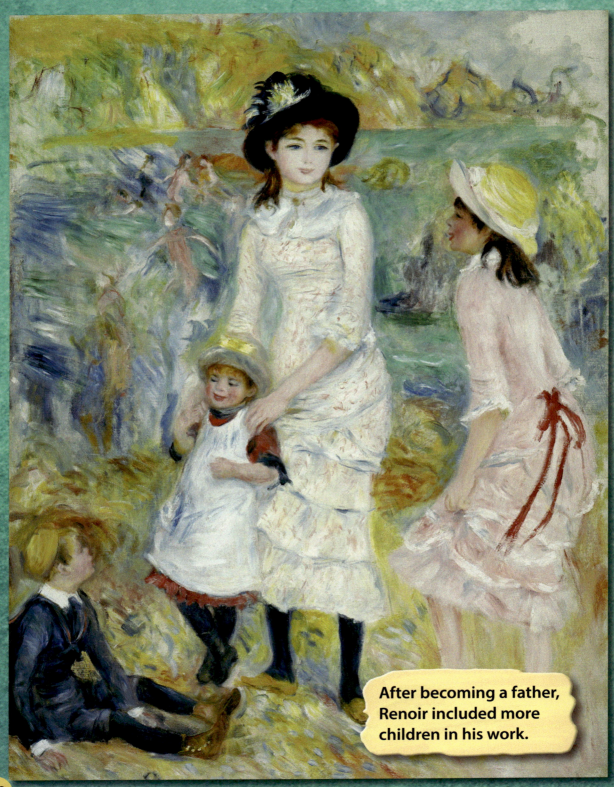

After becoming a father, Renoir included more children in his work.

CHAPTER 5

Home Sweet Home

The sun was beginning to set. Madame Renoir walked into the studio. "Daylight is fading, my dear," she said to her husband. "You do not want to tire yourself by working too long. Perhaps it is time to call it a day."

Monsieur Renoir agreed. He asked me to remove the brush from his hand. I carefully took it and placed it on the table. I set the palette next to it. Tomorrow, I would come back, just like I did every day. And Renoir would continue to paint on his canvas.

He was almost finished with his current painting. I stood next to him and looked at the painting on the easel.

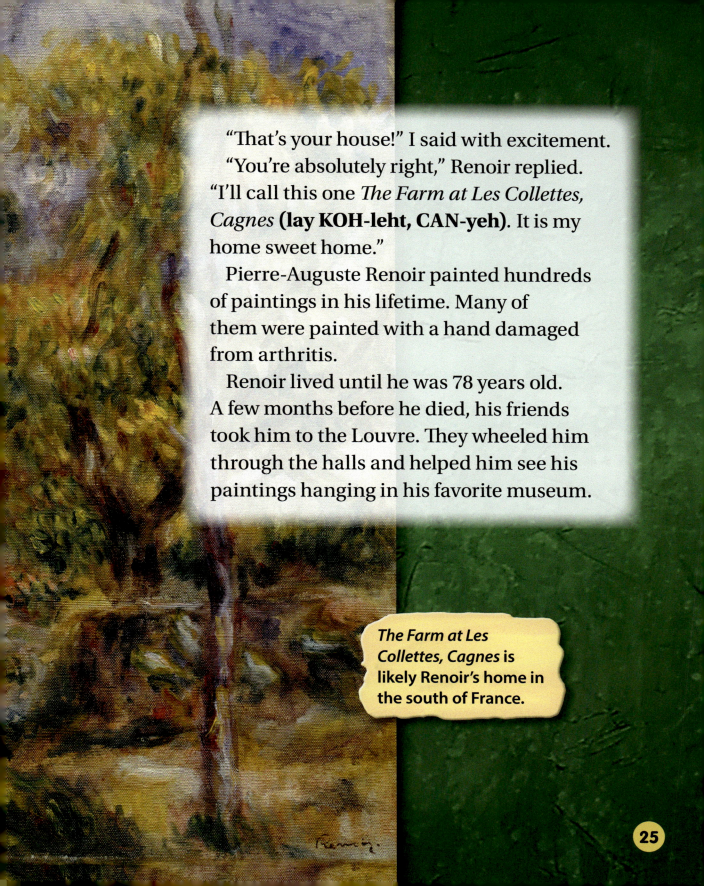

"That's your house!" I said with excitement.

"You're absolutely right," Renoir replied. "I'll call this one *The Farm at Les Collettes, Cagnes* **(lay KOH-leht, CAN-yeh)**. It is my home sweet home."

Pierre-Auguste Renoir painted hundreds of paintings in his lifetime. Many of them were painted with a hand damaged from arthritis.

Renoir lived until he was 78 years old. A few months before he died, his friends took him to the Louvre. They wheeled him through the halls and helped him see his paintings hanging in his favorite museum.

The Farm at Les Collettes, Cagnes is likely Renoir's home in the south of France.

Dance in the Country, 1883, and *The Theatre Box*, 1874 (right).

Timeline

1841   Pierre-Auguste Renoir is born on February 25 in Limoges **(lih-MOHJ)**, France.

1844   His family moves to Paris.

1854–1858   Renoir is apprenticed as a porcelain painter.

1860   Renoir visits the Louvre museum often and copies the artwork of the masters.

1862   Renoir takes art classes. He meets Claude Monet and Alfred Sisley **(SYS-lee)**.

1872   Renoir sells his first paintings to an art dealer.

1874   Renoir organizes an art show with Monet, Paul Cézanne **(say-ZAN)**, and Edgar Degas **(EHD-ger duh-GAH)**. Their artwork is given the name "impressionism."

1880   Renoir meets Aline Charigot, who acts as his model. He moves to Italy to study classical art.

1884   Renoir's art begins to look less like impressionism and more like classical Italian art.

1890   He marries Aline Charigot.

1897   Doctors tell Renoir he has arthritis. The disease injures his joints so that he has to use a wheelchair. He moves to Cagnes-sur-Mer **(CAN-yeh ser MEHR)** in the south of France.

1919   Renoir dies on December 3, at the age of 78.

Selected Works

1869	*La Grenouillére*
1870	*La Promenade*
1872	*Claude Monet Reading*
1874	*The Theatre Box*
1875	*The Skiff*
1876	*Dance at Le Moulin de la Galette*
1881	*Luncheon of the Boating Party*
1881	*Pink and Blue*
1881	*Two Sisters (On the Terrace)*
1881–1886	*The Umbrellas*
1883	*Dance in the Country*
1883	*Dance at Bougival*
1883	*By the Seashore*
1883	*Children on the Seashore, Guernsey*
1885	*The Umbrellas*
1893	*Young Girls at the Piano*
1905	*Young Woman Arranging Her Earring*
1908–1914	*The Farm at Les Collettes, Cagnes*
1918	*Madeleine Leaning on Her Elbow with Flowers in Her Hair*
1918–1919	*The Concert*
1918–1919	*The Bathers*
1919	*Landscape*

The Umbrellas took five years to paint, which is unusual for Renoir.

29

Further Works

Works Consulted

"Auguste Renoir (1841–1919)." *The Met.* Retrieved July 26, 2016. http://www.metmuseum.org/toah/hd/augu/hd_augu.htm

Covington, Richard. "Renoir's Controversial Second Act." *Smithsonian*, February 2010. Retrieved July 26, 2016. http://www.smithsonianmag.com/arts-culture/renoirs-controversial-second-act-4941803/

"Luncheon of the Boating Party." *The Philips Collection*. Retrieved July 26, 2016. https://www.phillipscollection.org/collection/luncheon-boating-party

Books

Cesar, Stanley. *Twenty-four Pierre-Auguste Renoir Paintings (Collection) for Kids*. Seattle: Amazon Digital Services, 2014.

Deiss, Susanna. *Renoir: The Magic of Childhood*. Scotts Valley: CreateSpace Independent Publishing Platform, 2013.

Sellier, Marie. *Renoir's Colors*. Los Angeles: J. Paul Getty Museum, 2010.

On the Internet

Biography: "Pierre-Auguste Renoir"
http://www.biography.com/people/pierre-auguste-renoir-20693609

Artsy Crafty Mom
https://artsycraftsymom.com/renoir-art-projects-for-kids/

Glossary

apprentice (uh-PREN-tis)—A young person who learns a skill from a master while working for little money.

arthritis (arth-RY-tus)—A disease that causes pain in the joints of the body.

brushstroke (BRUHSH-strohk)—The mark the paintbrush leaves with one movement.

canvas (KAN-vus)—Blank fabric on which many artists paint.

croissant (kruh-SAHNT)—A French roll that is buttery and flaky.

easel (EE-zul)—A stand or frame that holds an artist's canvas.

Impressionism (im-PREH-shuh-nism)—A style of painting that works with spots of color to capture a feeling more than an exact scene.

Louvre (LOOV)—A famous art museum in Paris, France.

madame (muh-DAHM)—"Missus" in French.

monsieur (mis-YUR)—"Mister" in French.

palette (PAL-et)—A thin oval board used for holding and mixing paints.

porcelain (POR-suh-lin)—A hard, shiny white material that is used to make dishes and decorations.

Seine (SEHN)—A river that runs through Paris.

skiff (skihf)—A small boat.

Index

apprentice 14
Argenteuil, France 18
arthritis 10, 25

canvas 23
Charigot, Aline (wife) 5, 7, 13, 17, 18, 23
Children on the Seashore, Guernsey 22
croissants 17

Dance at the Moulin de la Galette 20–21
Dance in the Country 26

easel 23

Farm at Les Collettes, Cagnes, The 24–25

Louvre 14, 25
Luncheon of the Boating Party 4–5

Monet, Claude 14, 17, 18–19
Monet Painting in His Garden at Argenteuil 18–19

palette 9, 10, 17, 23
Paris, France 14, 17
Pont Neuf, The 16
porcelain 14

Renoir, Pierre-Auguste
    apprenticeship 14
    childhood 14
    education 14
    friends 5, 14, 17, 18, 25
    porcelain painter 14
    studio 9, 13, 23
    study at the Louvre 14
    years in Paris 14, 17

Seine 17
Self-Portrait (1875) 8
Self-Portrait (1910) 11
Skiff, The 12–13

Theatre Box 27

Young Girls at the Piano 15

32